A Note From Rick Renner

I am on a personal quest to see a "revival of the Bible" so people can establish their lives on a firm foundation that will stand strong and endure the test as end-time storm winds begin to intensify.

In order to experience a revival of the Bible in your personal life, it is important to take time each day to read, receive, and apply its truths to your life. James tells us that if we will continue in the perfect law of liberty — refusing to be forgetful hearers, but determined to be doers — we will be blessed in our ways. As you watch or listen to the programs in this series and work through this corresponding study guide, I trust you will search the Scriptures and allow the Holy Spirit to help you hear something new from God's Word that applies specifically to your life. I encourage you to be a doer of the Word He reveals to you. Whatever the cost, I assure you — it will be worth it.

> Thy words were found, and I did eat them;
> and thy word was unto me the joy and rejoicing of mine heart:
> for I am called by thy name, O Lord God of hosts.
> — Jeremiah 15:16

Your brother and friend in Jesus Christ,

Rick Renner

Unless otherwise indicated, all scripture quotations are taken from the *King James Version* of the Bible.

Christ's Message to Smyrna

How To Use This Study Guide

This five-lesson study guide corresponds to *"Christ's Message to Smyrna" With Rick Renner* (Renner TV). Each lesson in this study guide covers a topic that is addressed during the program series, with questions and references supplied to draw you deeper into your own private study of the Scriptures on this subject.

To derive the most benefit from this study guide, consider the following:

First, watch or listen to the program prior to working through the corresponding lesson in this guide. (Programs can also be viewed at **renner.org** by clicking on the Media/Archives links or on our Renner Ministries YouTube channel.)

Second, take the time to look up the scriptures included in each lesson. Prayerfully consider their application to your own life.

Third, use a journal or notebook to make note of your answers to each lesson's Study Questions and Practical Application challenges.

Fourth, invest specific time in prayer and in the Word of God to consult with the Holy Spirit. Write down the scriptures or insights He reveals to you.

Finally, take action! Whatever the Lord tells you to do according to His Word, do it.

For added insights on this subject, it is recommended that you obtain Rick Renner's book *A Light in Darkness: Seven Messages to the Seven Churches.* You may also select from Rick's other available resources by placing your order at **renner.org** or by calling 1-800-742-5593.

TOPIC

Smyrna — A Place of Suffering

SCRIPTURES

1. **Revelation 2:8-11** — And unto the angel of the church in Smyrna write; These things saith the first and the last, which was dead, and is alive; I know thy works, and tribulation, and poverty, (but thou art rich) and I know the blasphemy of them which say they are Jews, and are not, but are the synagogue of Satan. Fear none of those things which thou shalt suffer: behold, the devil shall cast some of you into prison, that ye may be tried; and ye shall have tribulation ten days: be thou faithful unto death, and I will give thee a crown of life. He that hath an ear, let him hear what the Spirit saith unto the churches; He that overcometh shall not be hurt of the second death.

2. **Hebrews 10:34** — ...[You] took joyfully the spoiling of your goods, knowing in yourselves that ye have in heaven a better and an enduring substance.

GREEK WORDS

1. "I know" — **οἶδα** (*oida*): to see, perceive, understand, or comprehend; knowledge gained by personal experience or personal observation

2. "works" — does not appear in the oldest manuscripts

3. "tribulation" — **θλῖψις** (*thlipsis*): a burden that is crushing, debilitating, or overpowering; most often used in connection with displays of extreme hostility or torture

4. "poverty" — **πενία** (*penia*): pictures a person from a lower class who must perform manual labor to make a living; portrays a person capable of providing a meager income, but who doesn't own land or have investments for his future

5. "poverty" — **πτωχός** (*ptochos*): depicts abject poverty; total impoverishment; an appalling and horrifying level of poverty; a person so destitute that he is deprived of the barest essentials for living; pictures a homeless person who may have to scrounge to find enough food to

eat; a person whom society would consider down and out, financially ruined, and poverty-stricken

6. "spoiling" — ἁρπαγή (*harpage*): pillage; to seize, carry off, plunder, or confiscate

7. "goods" — ὑπάρχω (*huparcho*): to be in possession of physical possessions, financial resources, or property

SYNOPSIS

The five lessons in this study on *Christ's Message to Smyrna* will focus on the following topics:

- Smyrna — A Place of Suffering
- What Are True Riches?
- Persecution: How To Overcome It
- The Story of Polycarp
- A Message to Overcoming Believers

The emphasis of this lesson:

The church of Smyrna was a place of suffering for believers. Jesus was well aware of their faithful works, even in the midst of intense persecution. In spite of their abject poverty and what they lacked in the natural, they were abundantly rich spiritually.

The ancient city of Smyrna was a Roman province of Asia. Today, it is the city of Izmir in Turkey. In Smyrna, there were passageways underneath the marketplace. Historical records reveal that believers were often dragged into these passageways and tortured or even killed for their faith in ancient times. They were treated harshly by pagans for their righteous living and also by members of the Jewish community, who were upset because people were converting to Christianity. Indeed, Smyrna was a city of great suffering for believers.

How Pastors Are Like Angels

In Revelation 2:8, Christ began His message to the Church of Smyrna saying, "And unto the angel of the church in Smyrna write; These things saith the first and the last, which was dead, and is alive."

The word "angel" is the Greek word *angelos*, which describes *an angel or a specially designated messenger*. In this particular verse, the "angel" of the church referred to was *the pastor* of the church of Smyrna. When Christ spoke His message to the body of believers in Smyrna, He first communicated it to *the pastor*.

Whenever Jesus has something to say to a church, He always honors and works through spiritual authority. The pastor is the head, and his ears are always the first to hear what Jesus has to say — whether it is praise or correction. Jesus speaks His words to the pastor, who receives it, mulls it over, and disperses it to the people.

Your pastor is like an angel! He is a Heaven-sent blessing meant to provide leadership and a measure of guidance and direction for your life. It is really in your best interest to honor him, respect him, and pray for him regularly.

For Believers, Death Is Temporary

In Revelation 2:8, Jesus described Himself as "...the first and the last, which was dead, and is alive." The phrase "was dead" in Greek indicates *temporary death*. In other words, Jesus described His death as a brief interruption in His eternal existence — a temporary, short-lived pause. But now He is alive!

Remember, Christ was communicating a message of hope to a church that was undergoing suffering. At the start of His message, He immediately reminded the hearers that He, too, had suffered — even to the point of death. However, what He had gone through was extremely brief and temporary in light of eternity, and the same was true for them.

Believers in Smyrna were experiencing persecution, and some had been put to death by the Romans. Given the circumstances, these believers were undoubtedly worried about their futures and what would become of them. That is why Jesus let them know up front that even if they died, as He did, there was a promised resurrection to those who believe, and the pain of suffering would be only temporary.

Jesus Was 'in the Know'

Jesus continued in Revelation 2:9 saying, "I know thy works, and tribulation, and poverty, (but thou art rich) and I know the blasphemy of them which say they are Jews, and are not, but are the synagogue of Satan."

"I know" are the first two words Christ spoke, from the Greek word *oida*, which means *to see, perceive, understand, or fully comprehend*. It describes *knowledge gained by personal experience or personal observation*. "I know" (*oida*) is the same word Jesus used when He spoke to the church of Ephesus in Revelation chapter 2. Interestingly, the Greek structure of this verse actually says, "I know the works *of you*. I know *your unique works* that make you different from any of the other churches." Jesus was personally aware of every activity and deed that the believers in Smyrna were doing.

How did Jesus *see, fully comprehend*, and *personally observe* all that the believers in the church of Smyrna were going through? He walked in the very midst of the seven churches (*see* Revelation 2:1). What He learned about them was not secondhand information obtained from an angel or from someone's prayers. It was obtained by firsthand observation — Jesus had seen all their activities with His own eyes. This must have been a great encouragement for them to hear!

He Understood Their Tribulation

To what had Jesus been an eyewitness? Verse 9 says, "...thy works, and tribulation, and poverty...." The word "works" is the Greek word *erga*, which describes *the entirety of one's deeds, works, and activities*. Essentially, Jesus was saying, "I have personally been to your church and walked up and down the very center of it. I've seen everything that you've been doing, and I know absolutely everything about you."

Specifically, Jesus said He knew of their "tribulation." The word "tribulation" is the Greek word *thlipsis*, which describes *a burden that is crushing, debilitating, or overpowering*. Most often, this word is used in connection with *displays of extreme hostility or torture*.

Thlipsis (tribulation) was a favorite word used in Paul's writings. The earliest usage of this word was in the description of torture. Roman authorities would take a man who had been accused of some crime, and they would lay him flat on his back and bind him so that he couldn't move. He would be placed beneath a huge boulder which loomed above him. They would say to him, "If you don't confess the crime you've committed, we're going to drop this boulder on you."

Little by little, they would begin lowering the boulder toward the suspect criminal. The longer he held his tongue, the closer the boulder would creep toward him. Lower and lower it came until finally, the victim felt the full weight of the boulder pressing against him. Now he was under so much pressure and weight, he couldn't move. Suffocating and unable to breathe, if the victim would still not admit his crime, they would cut the rope, and the boulder would completely fall, crushing the individual.

This word *thlipsis* was used by Jesus as a visual representation of the mounting pressure the believers in Smyrna felt. It presents is a very clear picture of this Greek word translated here as "tribulation."

Jesus was personally fully aware of the debilitating, crushing situations the Christians in Smyrna were experiencing. Again, the Greek structure indicates that Jesus was saying, 'I intimately know the tribulations *of you — the specific, unique pressures and persecution you are enduring.* And I understand."

He Understood Their Poverty

Notice in Revelation 2:9, Jesus said, "I know thy works, and tribulation, and *poverty*…." Many scholars believe the word "poverty" describes the greatest form of tribulation the believers in Smyrna were facing. There are actually two words used for "poverty." The first is the Greek word *penia*, which pictures *a person from a lower class who must perform manual labor to make a living.* It portrays *a person capable of providing a meager income, but who doesn't own land or have investments for his future.* The word *penia* is not used for "poverty" in this verse.

The word "poverty" in this verse is the Greek word *ptochos*, which depicts *abject poverty.* It is *total impoverishment; an appalling and horrifying level of poverty in which a person is so destitute that he is deprived of the barest essentials for living.* This pictures *a homeless person who may have to scrounge to find enough food to eat — a person society would consider down and out, financially ruined, and poverty-stricken.* When Jesus told the church of Smyrna, "I know thy poverty," these were the conditions in which He had seen them living.

Many of the people who came to Christ in the First Century were lower-class slaves. We read about this in Ephesians 6:5, Colossians 3:22, Titus 2:9, and First Peter 2:18. Although slaves were accustomed to a lower standard of living, most of them had some form of income. This was not the case for the believers in Smyrna. They weren't just poor — they were living in complete impoverishment, scrounging around for food to eat. Poverty (*ptochos*) was the greatest form of tribulation they were suffering.

Why Were They So Poor?

The pagans in Smyrna believed that if you were financially blessed, it was a sign that the pagan gods were pleased with you. However, if you were poor, they believed it was a sign that the gods were punishing you for some reason. Accordingly, the poor were treated as social outcasts.

Most believers in Smyrna were suffering abject poverty due to persecution, but they were looked down upon as "the lowest of the low." They were being severely punished by the gods, and they were treated as social outcasts. What brought them into such "out of the ordinary poverty"?

In the city of Smyrna, there were trade guilds — what we might call labor unions today. A person who was a member of a trade guild was almost always guaranteed a job. But for those who were not trade-guild members, it was virtually impossible to find employment.

Trade guilds were notorious for pagan practices. Each guild had its own patron god who was worshiped at each gathering. Orgies, drunkenness, and idolatry were all activities that were a part of being in a trade guild. For Christians to be involved in such things would require them to deny Christ, forsake their faith, and violate their conscience. Any refusal to attend and participate in these pagan practices resulted in cancellation of membership and inability to secure future work.

Nevertheless, the believers in Smyrna chose to remain faithful to Christ and do what was right — regardless of the cost. Jesus knew the great sacrifices they had made and not only praised them for it, but also compensated them with "true riches."

STUDY QUESTIONS

Study to shew thyself approved unto God, a workman that needeth not to be ashamed, rightly dividing the word of truth.
— 2 Timothy 2:15

1. From cover to cover, the Bible talks about troubles and tribulations and the power of God and His Word to overcome them. Write out a scripture on this subject that has helped you trust God through tough times. (Consider Ephesians 4:11-15 and 2 Timothy 3:16, 17.)

2. The apostle Peter had much to say on the subject of suffering and how to navigate difficult times. Carefully read his insights in First Peter 5:6-10. What is the Holy Spirit telling you about your *response* and His *rewards*?

PRACTICAL APPLICATION

But be ye doers of the word, and not hearers only, deceiving your own selves.
—James 1:22

1. What is your understanding on the issue of suffering as a Christian? What might it include, and what does it *not* include?
2. Jesus told the believers in Smyrna, "I *know* thy works…" (Revelation 2:8). That is, He saw, understood, and gained knowledge of all their activities, deeds, and difficulties from *personal observation*. How does knowing that Jesus is personally aware of all *your* works and hardships — that He's right there with you — encourage you and strengthen your faith?
3. The tribulations we face often feel like the pressure of an immense boulder pressing against us. Describe the situation you're facing that is weighing on you with such great intensity. Take a moment to pour your heart out to God, inviting Him to work on your behalf.

LESSON 2

TOPIC

What Are True Riches?

SCRIPTURES

1. **Revelation 2:8, 9** — And unto the angel of the church in Smyrna write; These things saith the first and the last, which was dead, and is alive; I know thy works, and tribulation, and poverty, (but thou art rich) and I know the blasphemy of them which say they are Jews, and are not, but are the synagogue of Satan.
2. **Romans 16:16** — Salute one another with an holy kiss. The churches of Christ salute you.

GREEK WORDS

1. "rich" — πλούσιος (*plousios*): wealthy; pictures extreme wealth; could depict a person who isn't merely rich, but who is very rich

SYNOPSIS

The ancient city of Smyrna lies underneath the modern Turkish city of Izmir. At one time, Smyrna was a magnificent city in the Roman province of Asia — home to about 100,000 people during the time of the New Testament when the Church was being established there.

It was in Smyrna that the Agora — the largest marketplace in the entire Roman world — existed. The Agora consisted of three levels and was adorned with all kinds of sculptures and statues honoring the Roman gods and emperors. It was also the place where many Christians suffered terrible persecution in the ancient world — some even dying for their faith in the sight of pagan spectators. Yet in spite of all they endured, Jesus said that they were spiritually *rich*.

The emphasis of this lesson:

The believers in the city of Smyrna were terribly persecuted and lived in abject poverty as a result of their faith in Christ. Nevertheless, Jesus called them *rich*. They serve as an example that if you'll stand on God's Word and refuse to compromise, in the end you will always win.

What We've Learned So Far

Jesus had a message for the believers at the church of Smyrna. In delivering His message, He spoke to the "angel" of the church first (*see* Revelation 2:8). This "angel" — the Greek word *angelos* — was not a heavenly being. In this case, it was *a specially designated messenger*. Specifically, it was the *pastor* of the church of Smyrna. Christ honored the spiritual authority He established by speaking to the pastor first. It is the pastor's job to process the message from Jesus the Head of the Church and then deliver it to the congregation.

Jesus had been temporarily dead, but was made alive again. In Revelation 2:8, Jesus identified Himself as "...the first and the last, which was dead, and is alive." By saying He "was dead," Christ described His death as *temporary*. In the big picture of eternity, the duration of His death amounted to a brief pause or interruption — because He was made alive and is now alive forevermore.

Saying this was very important to the people in Smyrna because many believers were dying for their faith. Faced with such intense persecution, eternity was certainly on their minds. Essentially, Jesus encouraged them by saying, "I faced death, too, but know that it was only a temporary pause. There is a resurrection awaiting you and eternal life that follows."

Jesus knew their works. In Revelation 2:9, He said, "I know they works…." The word "know" is the Greek word *oida*, which means *to see, perceive, understand, or comprehend*. It is *knowledge gained by personal experience or personal observation*. When believers in Smyrna heard Jesus say, "I know (*oida*) thy works," they understood Him to say, "I have personally observed your church, walking up and down the midst of it. And what I know, I have seen with My own eyes."

The word "works" is the Greek word *erga*, which describes *the totality of a person's deeds, works, or activities*. When Jesus said, "I know thy works," a better translation would read, "I know everything there is to know about you — all your activities, deeds, and the hardships you've suffered. There is nothing about you that I do not know." This is also true of you. Jesus knows from personal observation everything there is to know about you.

Jesus knew their tribulation. The Greek structure of this verse actually means, "I know the tribulation *of you*. I know about the tribulation that is unique to you and different from every other church. No one else is going through what you're going through."

The word "tribulation" is the Greek word *thlipsis*, which describes *any situation that is crushing, debilitating, or overpowering*. It means anything that is *awful, critical, dire, dreadful, grave, grim*, or *humiliating*. "Tribulation" (*thlipsis*) is the word Jesus used to describe the mounting pressure He had personally seen the believers in Smyrna experiencing.

Jesus knew their poverty. As with the word tribulation, the Greek structure here indicates Jesus said, "I know the poverty *of you*. Other churches may be poor, but I am intimately aware of the unique condition of the poverty you are facing because of persecution."

The word "poverty" is the Greek word *ptochos*, which depicts *abject poverty or total impoverishment*. It is *an appalling and horrifying level of poverty,*

picturing a person so destitute that he is deprived of the barest essentials for liv-
ing. The word *ptochos* depicts *a homeless person who may have to scrounge to*
find enough food to eat. This is *a person society would consider down-and-out,*
financially ruined, or poverty-stricken.

The Far-Reaching Influence of Trade Guilds

The primary reason Christians in Smyrna were so utterly impoverished
was the influence of the trade guilds. There were guilds for painters, dyers,
weavers, tanners, teachers, doctors, bronze workers, goldsmiths, silver-
smiths, idol makers, and even slaves. To a great degree, the trade guilds
in the ancient world were so powerful that they determined the prices
of their goods and services and regulated everything about their trade in
their respective cities. If you were not a member of a guild, you couldn't
work. They operated on a "buddy system." When a new job became available, trade-guild members would make sure it went to a fellow member.

On the surface, it may seem trade guilds were good, but a closer look
reveals otherwise. Every meeting began with the worship of the pagan
patron god of that particular guild. Add to this idolatry, drunkenness, and
sexual debaucheries. There was one wicked vice after another — many
from which these Christians had recently been delivered.

This presented serious problems for believers in Smyrna, resulting in one
of two things: Believers either revoked their memberships from the trade
guilds, or the guilds revoked the memberships of the believers for refusing
to attend and participate in the activities. As these believers took a stand
for Christ, they lost their jobs in the process. They couldn't just go get
another job because the guilds controlled all employment opportunities.
Consequently, poverty became commonplace in Smyrna. Still, Jesus had
called these believers to a holy life. They knew they could no longer be a
part of trade guilds and subject themselves to such ungodly behavior. Thus,
they did the right thing, even though it was the hard thing.

Believers in Smyrna Were Compensated
With True Riches

Jesus had been in the very midst of the church of Smyrna and had personally witnessed the abject poverty they were experiencing for His sake. As a
result, Christ compensated them lavishly. In spite of their tribulation and
poverty, He said, "…But thou art rich…" (Revelation 2:9).

The word "rich" is the famous Greek word *plousios*, which means *wealthy*. It pictures *extreme, vast, abundant wealth — wealth so great it cannot be tabulated.* The word *plousios* is the very word used by Plato to describe *the wealth of the legendary King Midas.* No one at that time was richer than he was.

Interestingly, this is the word Jesus used to describe the church in Smyrna. Financially, they were struggling — but spiritually, they were opulent, and no one was richer than they were. This tells us that true riches are not always measured in money or material possessions. There are other kinds of riches.

Although the believers of Smyrna had been deprived of worldly goods, they were rich in other ways. Not having creature comforts or legal protection caused them to lean on each other. This produced a rich, meaningful level of fellowship among them that is less prevalent in countries where believers' rights are protected and the need for close-knit relationships isn't felt as intensely.

Christ's love permeated the members of this church in indescribable ways. The tenderness of the Holy Spirit was present whenever they came together. There was a depth of commitment between believers that was extraordinary. With genuine appreciation and love, they clung to Jesus and one another, experiencing a richness of covenant fellowship that was amazing.

They Were Rich in Genuine Affection

In Romans 16:16, the apostle Paul said, "Salute one another with an holy kiss...." To the Western mind, this may seem strange. However, it was not strange to members of the church of Smyrna.

Imagine the environment in which those early believers lived. Every time they left their church gathering, they never knew if they would see each other again. The person they were sitting next to could be killed before the next meeting. The uncertainty and danger caused believers to cherish what was most important — each other. So before they parted, they gave each other a kiss goodbye.

When they reconvened and saw one another again, there was great joy that their friends were still alive. They embraced and kissed each other. A holy kiss in this context describes an expression of euphoria that communicated, "You're still alive! You're still here!"

Clearly, the members of the church of Smyrna hardly had anything financially or materially. Yet they were abundantly rich in spiritual matters, including their level of fellowship with each other. Jesus said, "You are rich" — the Greek word *plousios*. No one was richer than they were.

Does this mean God wants you to live in abject poverty like the believers in Smyrna? Is it His will that you continually suffer financial lack? The answer is emphatically no. But He does want you to realize that if you're going through a hard time, don't measure your success by the dollars and cents you have. There are all kinds of riches awaiting you — a level of spiritual wealth like you have never known.

STUDY QUESTIONS

Study to shew thyself approved unto God, a workman that needeth not to be ashamed, rightly dividing the word of truth.
— 2 Timothy 2:15

1. Many times you will have to make the decision to do what's right rather than to please people and go against your conscience. What did the apostle Paul say about the importance of your conscience in Acts 24:16; First Timothy 1:5, 19; and Second Corinthians 1:12?

2. According to Romans 9:1, what is the connection between the Holy Spirit and your conscience? And what does First Timothy 4:1 and 2 identify as the danger of not listening to and keeping a clear conscience?

3. Have you sacrificed the comforts of this world to obey God? Have you gone without in order to see His Kingdom advanced in the lives of others? Read and write Jesus' promise to you in Matthew 19:29.

PRACTICAL APPLICATION

But be ye doers of the word, and not hearers only, deceiving your own selves.
— James 1:22

1. In your own words, how would you define *success*? And what does it mean to be *rich*?

2. How do you think God defines true success and true riches? In what ways do your definitions differ from His?

TOPIC

Encouragement for Your Hard Times — How To Overcome

SCRIPTURES

1. **Revelation 2:9, 10** — I know thy works, and tribulation, and poverty, (but thou are rich) and I know the blasphemy of them which say they are Jews, and are not, but are the synagogue of Satan. Fear none of those things which thou shalt suffer: behold, the devil shall cast some of you into prison, that ye may be tried; and ye shall have tribulation ten days: be thou faithful unto death, and I will give thee a crown of life.

2. **John 1:5** — And the light shineth in darkness; and the darkness comprehended it not.

GREEK WORDS

1. "fear" — **φόβος** (*phobos*): fear, fright, or terror

2. "none" — **μηδὲν** (*meden*): means none at all, not a speck, not any; a word that demands the immediate halt of something already in progress

3. "shalt" — **μέλλω** (*mello*): sets forth the idea of events that have yet to occur, as opposed to events that have already occurred or that are presently taking place.

4. "suffer" — **πάσχω** (*pascho*): to be negatively affected by something

5. "behold" — **ἰδοὺ** (*idou*): to look; pictures amazement, shock, and wonder

6. "devil" — **διάβολος** (*diabolos*): slanderous; pictures one who repetitiously throws accusations at someone, striking again and again; depicts the activity of one who incessantly accuses and slanders some-

one or who continually brings allegations, assertions, charges, claims, or indictments against someone

7. "shall cast" — βάλλω (*ballo*): to hurl or to throw

8. "prison" — φυλακή (*phulake*): a Roman prison, one of the most dreadful, fearsome places in the Roman world

9. "tried" — πειράζω (*peiradzo*): to test; pictures a calculated test deliberately designed to expose any deficiency

10. "tribulation" — θλῖψις (*thlipsis*): a burden that is crushing, debilitating, or overpowering; most often used in connection with displays of extreme hostility or torture

11. "comprehended" — καταλαμβάνω (*katalambano*): to seize; to grab hold of; to pull down; to tackle; to conquer; to master; to hold under one's power

12. "be thou" — γίνομαι (*ginomai*): to become; depicts a process of becoming

13. "faithful" — πιστός (*pistos*): conveys the idea of people who are faithful, reliable, loyal, and steadfast

14. "unto" — ἄχρι (*achri*): up to; as far as; or including

15. "death" — θάνατος (*thanatos*): the physical state of death; in the New Testament, it also depicts mortal danger, a dangerous circumstance, or something that is fatal; in the Roman legal system, it described the death penalty

SYNOPSIS

Scholars believe the church of Smyrna was established during the time Paul was living in Ephesus. It seems he dispatched ministry workers to Smyrna to preach, teach, and win souls to Christ. Yet the believers there faced terrible persecution from the outset. The city was devoted to idolatry and the worship of pagan deities, and the emerging church was subject to much tribulation — predominantly in the area of poverty due to their unwillingness to fit in with the trade guilds that could secure their livelihoods.

In the center of the city of Smyrna was the Agora — the largest marketplace in all of the entire Roman Empire. History reveals that believers were dragged into the passageways and open courtyards of the Agora and publicly persecuted. Some were officially tried by the proconsul of the city and then executed for their faith. Indeed, Smyrna had a reputation for being a place of suffering.

The emphasis of this lesson:

The true riches Christ offers us are abundant and spiritual in nature. Abject poverty was the widespread form of persecution the early believers in Smyrna faced. Yet, in spite of their poverty, Jesus called them *rich*. He also warned them of the specific trouble the devil was about to bring against them. But Jesus also comforted them that they were not to fear because the duration of that troublesome time would be limited.

Poverty Was Smyrna's Primary Form of Tribulation

Jesus told the Church at Smyrna, "I know thy works, and tribulation, and poverty..." (Revelation 2:9). Of all the tribulation the believers in Smyrna was experiencing, poverty was most common. The word "poverty" is the Greek word *ptochos*, which depicts *abject poverty or total impoverishment*. It is *an appalling and horrifying level of poverty in which a person is so destitute that he is deprived of the barest essentials for living*. It pictures *a homeless person who may have to scrounge to find enough food to eat — a person society would consider down and out, financially ruined, and poverty-stricken.*

We've learned that the cause for this widespread poverty was the result of believers' losing their jobs and being unable to secure new work. Trade guilds in Smyrna dominated the workforce. If you were a trade-guild member, you had no problem getting work and maintaining a steady income. If you were not in a guild, you were blacklisted from all employment.

Trade guilds were saturated with ungodly pagan practices. Each guild had its own patron god, and at each meeting, members worshiped this god, which involved drunkenness and participation in orgies. For these reasons, many believers terminated their membership in their respective guilds. Others simply quit attending trade-guild meetings, causing guild leaders to revoke believers' memberships.

When people in Smyrna came to Christ, they made a decision to submit to His lordship and say no to the practices of the trade guilds. When they said no, they lost their jobs. The unbelieving pagans didn't understand the believers' new faith, so they criticized and persecuted them.

Meanwhile, the Jewish community also disliked believers because the Christian faith provided competition to Judaism. Hence, the Jewish community stirred up all kinds of trouble for believers whenever they had the chance. The persecution from the Jews was so bad that Jesus called the religious leaders in Smyrna "the synagogue of Satan" (*see* Revelation 2:9). Thus, trials and troubles came against believers from *multiple* sources, but the worst of all their tribulations was severe financial distress.

Jesus Called These Believers 'Rich'

In spite of all the dire hardships Christians in Smyrna were facing, Jesus called them "rich" (Revelation 2:9). This word "rich" is the Greek word *plousios*, and it describes *one that is wealthy and fabulously rich* — we might say *"filthy, stinking rich."* It pictures *extreme, vast wealth.* This word was used by Plato to describe the wealth of the legendary King Midas — the king considered to be the richest man in the world during his lifetime.

On one hand, believers were financially and materially experiencing severe poverty. They had taken a stand for their faith in Christ, deciding to listen to their conscience and not participate in the ungodly practices of the trade guilds. As a result, they lost their jobs and were unable to secure work. On the other hand, they were fabulously rich in fellowship with the Lord and with each other.

At times the believers' homes were plundered and they were harassed by local mobs. When this happened, they had to choose their pain: go to the police or government officials and risk the likelihood of being arrested and thrown in jail for their faith. *Or* they could deal with the pain of the circumstances. Since they were rich in covenant fellowship with each other, they opted to draw assistance and strength from fellow believers.

The believers in Smyrna learned to lean on one another for life-sustaining support. What they lost in finances and material possessions, they gained spiritually and relationally.

Fifteen Riches for New Testament Believers

Riches are not always measured in dollars and cents. There are extraordinary riches available to us as believers that far outweigh and overshadow monetary means.

In what ways are we as believers spiritually rich?

1. We have *riches in Heaven*. (Matthew 6:20 and Luke 12:33)
2. We are blessed with the *riches of fellowship*. (Acts 20:32)

3. We have the fabulous *riches of God's kindness*. (Romans 2:4)

4. The *riches of God's power* dwell inside us. (2 Corinthians 4:7)

5. We have the *riches of a generous spirit*. (2 Corinthians 9:10; 11:6)

6. The untold *riches of God's glory* belong to us. (Ephesians 1:18; Philippians 4:19; Colossians 1:27)

7. We possess the *riches of God's bountiful mercy*. (Ephesians 2:4)

8. We're heirs to the *riches of His grace*. (Ephesians 1:7, 8; 2:7)

9. We are partakers of the *riches of Christ*. (Ephesians 2:8)

10. We have the *riches of the fellowship of the Holy Spirit*. (Philippians 2:1)

11. We're blessed with the *riches of the saints and their partnership*. (Colossians 1:12)

12. We have the *riches of wisdom and knowledge*. (Colossians 2:2, 3)

13. We have the *riches of a good foundation for the future* laid up for us. (1 Timothy 6:19)

14. We have the abundant *riches of faith*. (James 2:5)

15. The imperishable *riches of eternal reward* are stored up for us in Heaven. (1 Peter 1:4)

These are *true riches*, and they are priceless! Realize that some of the poorest churches in history have been the most spiritually rich, even though God wanted better for them. Similarly, some of the financially richest churches in history have been spiritually poor, but they didn't have to be.

Jesus Said, 'Fear None of Those Things'

Jesus continued His message to the church of Smyrna in Revelation 2:10 saying, "Fear none of those things which thou shalt suffer: behold, the devil shall cast some of you into prison, that ye may be tried; and ye shall have tribulation ten days: be thou faithful unto death, and I will give thee a crown of life."

First, notice He said, "Fear none of those things…." The word "fear" is the Greek word *phobos*, which describes *fright, terror, or panic*. When Jesus said, "Fear none of those things," He was saying, "Don't give place to fear, terror, or panic." Panic was trying to grip the believers in Smyrna because of what they were experiencing and what they saw coming. Jesus told them to put a halt to fear.

Actually, the Greek structure in this verse could be translated: "Stop fearing. Stop it and stop it now." This was a command to put a halt to the spirit of fear operating in their lives. Giving in to fear never helps — it only harms. An *RIV* translation of Revelation 2:10 says, Don't give place to fear, terror, or panic. Stop fearing and stop it now. Put a halt to fear, terror, and panic operating in your life...."

This is precisely why throughout the New Testament, Jesus, the Holy Spirit, and angels told people again and again to "fear not." A few examples in Scripture include: Matthew 14:25-27; 17:1-7; Mark 5:35, 36; 6:47-50; Luke 5:1-10; 8:41-50; and Acts 18:4-9; 27:19-24. Every time we are told, "Fear not," it means, "Stop it and stop it now. Put a halt to fear, terror, and panic operating in your life."

What Is the Meaning of 'Shalt Suffer'?

Next, Jesus said, "Thou shalt suffer." The word "shalt" is the Greek word *mello*, and it sets forth the idea of *events that have yet to occur*. Even though the believers in Smyrna had been through quite a bit already, Jesus was giving them a forewarning: "The battle isn't over." It was a similar forewarning to the warning He gives all believers in John 16:33, "...In the world ye shall have tribulation." Thankfully, Jesus also says, "...But be of good cheer, I have overcome the world."

Jesus has given us the empowering gift of the Holy Spirit, and John 16:13 says one of the Spirit's jobs is to *show us things to come*. Instead of letting events suddenly occur and take us by surprise, the Holy Spirit will reveal to us ahead of time what is coming. Our job is to open our ears and be willing to listen to what He says. He will show us both the good and the difficult things on the horizon.

The Holy Spirit shows us the future not to scare us, but to *prepare* us. He wants us to be spiritually, mentally, and emotionally prepared. This is why He forewarned the believers in Smyrna. He was preparing them for the future things they would "suffer."

The word "suffer" is the Greek word *pascho*, which simply means *to be negatively affected by something*. Jesus was forewarning the church of Smyrna, "You're going to experience some negative things in the days ahead, but fear none of those things. Don't be afraid. Put a halt to fear's operation in your life. Everything is going to be all right." Jesus' message to Smyrna is good spiritual insight for us too.

The Specific Details of What Was Coming

Then Jesus told the believers some specific details of what was coming. In Revelation 2:10 He said, "…Behold, the devil shall cast some of you into prison, that ye may be tried and ye shall have tribulation ten days: be thou faithful unto death, and I will give thee a crown of life" (Revelation 2:10). Notice the meanings of some of the key words and phrases in this verse.

The Devil: The word "devil" is the Greek word *diabolos*, and here it actually describes *what* is going to happen. "Devil" means *one who slanders or one who repetitiously throws accusations at someone, striking again and again*. It depicts the activity of *one who incessantly accuses and slanders someone or who continually brings allegations, assertions, charges, claims, or indictments against someone*.

Jesus essentially forewarned the church of Smyrna, "The devil himself is going to begin working in your community through people and circumstances, bringing allegations, suspicions, misunderstandings, and charges against you." The pagans in Smyrna didn't understand the Christian faith, and what people don't understand, they tend to attack and tear apart.

Shall Cast Into Prison: The phrase "shall cast" is from the word *ballo*, which means *to hurl or throw*. It describes *very fast movement*. Jesus said, "They're going to hurl or throw some of you into prison very fast." The word "prison" is the Greek word *phulake*, which describes *a Roman prison — one of the most dreadful, fearsome places in the Roman world*. When people were thrown into a Roman prison, they often remained there. It was usually the equivalent of a death sentence.

That Ye May Be Tried: The word "tried" is the Greek word *peiradzo*. It describes *a calculated test deliberately designed to expose any deficiency*. The devil "tried" Jesus in the wilderness during the 40 days He fasted. The enemy did everything he could to break Jesus and get Him to compromise His identity as the Son of God. Likewise, the devil "tried" the church of Smyrna, casting many of them into prison and causing tribulation.

Tribulation: Jesus told the believers, "…Ye shall have tribulation." The word "tribulation" is the Greek word *thlipsis*, which describes *a burden that is crushing, debilitating, or overpowering*. Then Jesus added two wonderful words to His forewarning: *ten days*. Why did He add the words "ten days"? He said this to signify that the imprisonment would be for *a limited period of time*.

Yes, there are other meanings to this phrase "ten days," but what is important to understand is that their suffering wouldn't last forever. It would happen for a limited period of time. Jesus was saying, "If you'll be faithful and endure to the end, you'll get beyond all of this. It's only going to last for a short time."

You may be going through a very troubling time right now, but Jesus wants you to know it won't last forever. There is an expiration date on your difficulties. The devil is the one behind your suffering, not God. If you will stand your ground, be true to your faith, and not give in to the circumstances the enemy is orchestrating, eventually you will overcome!

STUDY QUESTIONS

**Study to shew thyself approved unto God, a workman that needeth
not to be ashamed, rightly dividing the word of truth.
— 2 Timothy 2:15**

1. One of the greatest blessings of being in a relationship with the Holy Spirit is hearing His voice. Take a moment to read Jesus' words in John 14:26 and John 16:13, along with Psalm 25:14 and Amos 3:7. What is the common theme promised in these passages?
2. Take time to write down the 15 fabulous riches that are yours through Christ Jesus. Which of these spiritual treasures can you see operating in your life?

PRACTICAL APPLICATION

**But be ye doers of the word, and not hearers only,
deceiving your own selves.
— James 1:22**

1. Have you or someone close to you suffered abuse or mistreatment because of faith in Christ? Have you suffered loss on your job, in your community, or in your family? If so, briefly share your experience. How is this study on Christ's message to Smyrna encouraging you?
2. In Revelation 2:10, Jesus instructed the believers in Smyrna to "be faithful unto death," which actually means "Be *in the process of becoming faithful* unto death."

Stop and take a personal inventory of where God has placed you. What practical steps can you take today to *be more faithful?*

- **In your home** (including your family relationships)
- **On your job** (including your relationships with your boss and coworkers)
- **At your church** (including your relationships with your pastor and other church members)

TOPIC

The Story of Polycarp

SCRIPTURES

1. **Revelation 2:8-10** — And unto the angel of the church in Smyrna write; These things saith the first and the last, which was dead, and is alive; I know thy works, and tribulation, and poverty, (but thou art rich) and I know the blasphemy of them which say they are Jews, and are not, but are the synagogue of Satan. Fear none of those things which thou shalt suffer: behold, the devil shall cast some of you into prison, that ye may be tried; and ye shall have tribulation ten days: be thou faithful unto death, and I will give thee a crown of life.

2. **Hebrews 11:35-38** — ...And others were tortured, not accepting deliverance; that they might obtain a better resurrection: and others had trial of cruel mockings and scourgings, yea, moreover of bonds and of imprisonment: they were stoned, they were sawn asunder, were tempted, were slain with the sword: they wandered about in sheepskins and goatskins; being destitute, afflicted, tormented.... They wandered in deserts, and in mountains, and in dens and caves of the earth.

GREEK WORDS

1. "tortured" — τυμπανίζω (*tumpanidzo*): to torture; refers to a wheel-shaped instrument of torture over which criminals were stretched as though they were skins and then horribly beaten with clubs or thongs

2. "mockings" — ἐμπαίζω (*empaidzo*): to play a game; often used for playing a game with children or for amusing a crowd by impersonating someone in a silly and exaggerated way; might be used in a game of charades when someone intends to comically portray someone or even to make fun of, ridicule, or mock someone

3. "scourgings" — μάστιξ (*mastix*): a word borrowed from the world of torture; denoted the act of recurrently beating a prisoner or victim; once a person's wounds had mended, the torturers brought him back to the whipping post, where he was struck again and again; such beatings were sporadic, but constant, and although they were not usually serious enough to kill, they kept a victim in constant pain and misery; it was torment and abuse, a scourge that caused great suffering and prolonged anguish; it also depicts a recurring sickness or physical affliction that keeps a sufferer in a protracted, repetitive state of suffering

4. "bonds" — δεσμός (*desmos*): chains, bonds; pictures that which binds

5. "imprisonments" — φυλακή (*phulake*): a Roman prison, one of the most dreadful, fearsome places in the Roman world

6. "stoned" — λιθάζω (*lithadzo*): to stone; to overwhelm or bury with stones; to assail with stones with the intention to kill

7. "sawn asunder" — πρίζω (*pridzo*): to saw; to cut into two pieces; pictures the horrible practice of sawing in half

8. "tempted" — πειράζω (*peiradzo*): to put to the test; depicts a test to expose the truth about the quality of a substance; an intense examination or questioning; an interrogation

9. "slain" (by the sword) — φόνος (*phonos*): to slaughter; to massacre; pictures butchery and carnage

10. "wandered" — περιέρχομαι (*perierchomai*): to wander; to roam; to move around;

11. "sheepskins and goatskins" — could refer to clothing or Nero's brutal killing of believers

12. "destitute" — ὑστερέω (*hustereo*): to be lacking; depleted; impoverished; suffering physical need

13. "afflicted" — θλίβω (*thlibo*): to be pressured; compressed; suffocated

14. "tormented" — κακουχέω (*kakoucheo*): to oppress; to treat evilly; to torment; to maltreat; to have it badly

15. "wandering" — **πλανάω** (*planao*): to wander; roaming, perhaps due to being deliberately misled

16. "deserts" — **ἔρημος** (*eremos*): pictures a deserted place; a remote spot, a place that was out of the way; somewhere off the beaten track; an obscure site

17. "mountains" — **ὄρος** (*oros*): a mountain or a hill

18. "dens" — **ὀπή** (*ope*): holes in the earth, usually in remote locations

19. "caves" — **σπήλαιον** (*spelaion*): dens; caves; caverns; hiding places

20. "I know" — **οἶδα** (*oida*): to see, perceive, understand, or comprehend; knowledge gained by personal experience or personal observation

21. "works" — does not appear in the oldest manuscripts

22. "tribulation" — **θλῖψις** (*thlipsis*): a burden that is crushing, debilitating, or overpowering; most often used in connection with displays of extreme hostility or torture

23. "poverty" — **πτωχός** (*ptochos*): Depicts abject poverty; total impoverishment; an appalling and horrifying level of poverty; a person so destitute that he is deprived of the barest essentials for living; pictures a homeless person who may have to scrounge to find enough food to eat; a person society would consider down and out, financially ruined, and poverty-stricken

24. "fear" — **φόβος** (*phobos*): fear, fright, or terror

25. "none" — **μηδὲν** (*meden*): means none at all, not a speck, not any; a word that demands the immediate halt of something already in progress

26. "shalt" — **μέλλω** (*mello*): it sets forth the idea of events that have yet to occur, as opposed to events that have already occurred in the past or that are presently taking place.

27. "suffer" — **πάσχω** (*pascho*): to be negatively affected by something

28. "behold" — **ἰδοὺ** (*idou*): to look; pictures amazement, shock, and wonder

29. "devil" — **διάβολος** (*diabolos*): slanderous; pictures one who repetitiously throws accusations at someone, striking again and again; depicts the activity of one who incessantly accuses and slanders someone or who continually brings allegations, assertions, charges, claims, or indictments against someone

30. "shall cast" — **βάλλω** (*ballo*): to hurl or to throw

31. "prison" — **φυλακή** (*phulake*): a Roman prison, one of the most dreadful, fearsome places in the Roman world

32. "tried" — **πειράζω** (*peiradzo*): to test; pictures a calculated test deliberately designed to expose any deficiency

33. "comprehended" — **καταλαμβάνω** (*katalambano*): to seize; to grab hold of; to pull down; to tackle; to conquer; to master; to hold under one's power

34. "be thou" — **γίνομαι** (*ginomai*): to become; depicts a process of becoming

35. "faithful" — **πιστός** (*pistos*): conveys the idea of people who are faithful, reliable, loyal, and steadfast

36. "unto" — **ἄχρι** (*achri*): unto; up to; as far as; including

37. "death" — **θάνατος** (*thanatos*): the physical state of death; in the New Testament, it also depicts mortal danger, a dangerous circumstance, or something that is fatal; in the Roman legal system, it described the death penalty

SYNOPSIS

The city of Smyrna was located in the Roman province of Asia, where the Turkish city of Izmir now stands. In the early New Testament period, some believe it was home to about 100,000 people. During that time, there was a Christian church in the city that had been planted by the efforts of associates of Paul.

The church of Smyrna experienced much persecution. Believers were not only harassed and tortured in the passageways of the Agora, they were also persecuted in the city's ancient stadium. One believer martyred for his faith was a man by the name of Polycarp. It was in the Smyrna stadium over 2,000 years ago that Polycarp remained true to his faith and died victoriously in the power of God.

The emphasis of this lesson:

Polycarp was a notable believer who lived a long life, serving the believers in the city of Smyrna. At the close of his life, he laid down his life in honor of Christ. He was faithful to the end and left this world in a blaze of God's power.

The Master Was Well Aware
of the Believers' Misery

In Revelation 2:9, Jesus spoke a message to the church of Smyrna, saying, "I know thy works, and tribulation, and poverty, (but thou art rich)...." We have learned that the phrase "I know" is the Greek word *oida*, which means *to see, perceive, understand, or gain knowledge by personal experience or personal observation*. The word "works" is the Greek word *erga*, which is an all-encompassing word describing *all a person's actions, deeds, and activities*.

When you put these words together, Jesus' statement, "I know thy works" means, "There's nothing about you that I do not know. I've seen everything with My own eyes. What I know has not been told to Me by someone else in prayer or reported to Me by an angel. I've been in the very midst of your church and I've observed you — your deeds, your activities, and everything about you."

Then, Jesus specifically described two things He had seen: their "tribulation" and their "poverty." The word "tribulation" is the Greek word *thlipsis*, which means *a burden that is crushing, debilitating, or overpowering*. It describes *a high-pressure situation that is decimating and suffocating*. The word "poverty" is the Greek word *ptochos*, which indicates *abject poverty* or *total impoverishment*. It amplifies the word "tribulation" to really let us know what the believers in Smyrna were going through.

They Made a Clean Break
From Pagan Practices

The reason the believers in Smyrna were financially destitute and suffering lack was that they had lost their jobs. Once they became Christians, they would no longer take part in the pagan practices of their employers and coworkers. In Smyrna, everyone was a member of a trade guild, and as members, they worshiped the patron god of their guild and participated in drunkenness and sexual debauchery in their meetings.

Believers could no longer in good conscience be committed to Christ and continue in such ungodly behavior. Therefore, they either canceled their memberships or their memberships were revoked by the trade guild for failing to attend and participate in meetings. Employment opportunities were only given to those who were in a trade guild, so after believers' memberships were lost, they were out of work and couldn't secure employment elsewhere.

Although the church of Smyrna was experiencing other forms of tribulation, "poverty" was being experienced by virtually every believer. Their decision to follow and obey Christ resulted in financial and material lack.

Opposition From the Jews

Historically, there was a large Jewish community in Smyrna. They became very upset with the new Christian sect because many of the Jews were converting to Christianity. As a result, Jewish leaders began creating suspicions and circulating rumors about Christians among the pagan population, causing them to have bad sentiments toward believers.

Jesus said their behavior was so deplorable that they were of the "synagogue of Satan" (Revelation 2:9). The word "Satan" is the Greek word *satanas*, which means *one who accuses, one who slanders*. The Jewish leaders were in partnership with Satan himself, doing his dirty work of slandering and accusing God's people.

Nevertheless, Jesus told the believers, "Fear none of those things which thou shalt suffer..." (Revelation 2:10).

Forewarned To *Prepare*, Not To *Scare*

The word "fear" is the Greek word *phobos*, which describes *fear, fright, or terror*. The word "none" is the Greek word *meden*, which means *none at all, not a speck, not any*. It is a word that also demands *the immediate halt of something already in progress*. This word *meden* ("none") and its tense would only be used if people were already in a state of panic, and that is what the believers in Smyrna were experiencing.

Revelation 2:10 depicts Jesus like a military commander. As the Head of the Church, He spoke to the believers in Smyrna and basically said, "Stop fearing, and stop it now. Put a halt to fear. In fact, I prohibit the operation of fear. There's simply no room for it here." Jesus knew that fear has no profit at all, so He told them, "Fear none of those things which thou shalt suffer."

Here we see Jesus speaking the truth in love like He always does. He didn't sugarcoat the situation and say, "Everything is going to be fine, and you're never going to have any problems." Instead, He told them the truth, forewarning them of the difficulties ahead. His love was displayed in His preparation of the believers for what was coming.

The word "shalt" in verse 10 is the Greek word *mello*, and it describes *something that's coming*. It sets forth *the idea of events that have yet to occur.* Although the church in Smyrna had already been through a lot, Jesus was telling them, "There is more trouble ahead that you're going to suffer." The word "suffer" is the Greek word *pascho*, which means *to be negatively affected by something — circumstances that bring negative consequences.* In His love for the believers in Smyrna, Christ forewarned them *to prepare* them, not *to scare* them.

Christ Unveiled the Details of the Attack

In Revelation 2:10, Jesus continued by saying, "...Behold, the devil shall cast some of you into prison, that ye may be tried; and ye shall have tribulation ten days: be thou faithful unto death, and I will give thee a crown of life" (Revelation 2:10).

First, notice the word "behold" — the Greek word *idou*, which is almost impossible to translate. Essentially, it means *to look in amazement, shock, and wonder.* It is an exclamation of, "Wow!" By using *idou* ("behold"), it gives the idea of Jesus being extremely impressed with what He is about to say. It was as if He was saying, "Wow! It is amazing what the devil's going to try to do to you, but he will not ultimately prevail." (Jesus uses this same word *idou*, translated "behold," in Mathew 28:20 and Luke 10:19).

Then Jesus said, "The devil will cast some of you into prison...." The word "devil" is the Greek word *diabolos*, and with it is a definite article, which indicates that this is not just a little demonic activity — it is the devil himself. *Diabolos* literally means *one who repetitiously throws accusations, allegations, charges, and claims at someone, striking again and again.* This definition actually describes how the believers were going to be attacked.

Through the continuous slander of others, some of the believers would be "cast into prison." The word "cast" is the Greek word *ballo*, which means *to hurl or throw*, and the word "prison" is the Greek word *phulake*, which describes *a Roman prison* — one of the most dreadful, fearsome places in the Roman world. Landing in a Roman prison was like receiving a death sentence, and this is what Jesus forewarned the believers in Smyrna that the devil was about to do to some of them.

Why was the devil about to throw these people in prison? It was so that they could be "tried." The word "tried" is the Greek word *peiradzo*, which pictures *a calculated test deliberately designed to expose any deficiency or to break something*. The Christians in Smyrna had made a commitment to the lordship of Jesus. They vowed to serve Him regardless of the cost. Their finances, material possessions, and jobs were not more important than their relationship with Him.

By using the word "tried," Jesus was warning the believers that Satan had devised a calculated test to see how serious they were about their faith. He was going to hurl some of them into prison to break them so they would recant their commitment to Christ. This is the same strategy Satan uses against you — he will even try to make you believe God is behind all the problems in your life. Nothing could be further from the truth.

Jesus then added, "…and ye shall have tribulation ten days…" (Revelation 2:10). The word "tribulation" is again the Greek word *thlipsis*, which describes *a crushing, debilitating, or overpowering situation*. Thankfully, Jesus said it would only be for "ten days." This time frame may have symbolically referred to the ten Roman emperors who persecuted the Church, but it more likely signified that the persecution wouldn't last forever.

Jesus Said, 'Be Thou Faithful'

"Be thou faithful unto death" is what Jesus instructed them to do. The phrase "be thou" is the Greek word *ginomai*, which means *to become*, and it depicts *a process of becoming*. In other words, Jesus was saying, "Work on becoming more faithful where you are today. Put all your energy into it, and be faithful — even unto death if necessary."

The Greek meaning of "be thou faithful unto death" could actually be translated, "Be thou *in the process* of becoming faithful." It signifies starting right where you are and building faithfulness into your life today. When tomorrow comes, build on it again by proving yourself faithful, and do the same thing the next day. It is an ongoing construction project. The more faithfulness you construct in your character, the less difficult it will be to be faithful when times get tough.

Just like the believers in Smyrna, we are to be faithful "unto death." The word "unto" is the Greek word *achri*, which means *up to, as far as, or including*. The word "death" is the Greek word *thanatos*, and it describes *the physical state of death*. In the New Testament, it also depicts *mortal danger*, *a dangerous circumstance*, or *something that is fatal*. In the Roman legal system, it described *the death penalty*. Regardless of what we are facing, Jesus wants us to work on becoming more faithful each day.

Polycarp Was Faithful

There is one notable believer in Smyrna who took Jesus' words to heart, and his name was Polycarp. Although Polycarp had been born into a pagan home, he was adopted by a Christian woman when he was a child and raised in the ways of God. He had such a profound love for the Lord that it even came to the attention of the apostle John who lived in nearby Ephesus.

History records that John came to Smyrna, laid hands on Polycarp, and ordained him into the ministry. From then on, Polycarp's entire life was spent serving God's people. He first served as a deacon, then a pastor, and ultimately he became the bishop of the church of Smyrna. The Jews hated Polycarp because he was leading the new Christian sect that was causing many Jews to leave Judaism and convert to Christianity.

To retaliate, the Jewish leaders in the synagogue in Smyrna began to stir up problems. They circulated stories blaming the Christians for bad weather, crop failures, and every other problem imaginable. At that time, Polycarp was the most visible Christian in the city. According to tradition, when he was 86 years old and living on the outskirts of town, there was a knock on his door. When he answered, he was met by a group of Roman soldiers who had come to arrest him for his faith.

He was such a kind and benevolent man that he invited the soldiers into his house and before they took him away, he gave them something to drink and served them a meal. While they ate, he ministered to them, seizing the opportunity to share Christ with his accusers.

Shortly thereafter, they brought him before the proconsul in Smyrna, who commanded him to renounce his faith and to return to paganism. Early Christian writers record that Polycarp said to the proconsul, "Eighty-six years I have been His servant, and He has done me no wrong. How can I blaspheme my King who saved me?"

So the proconsul ordered that he be burned at the stake. Thus, more than 2,000 years ago, Polycarp was dragged into the stadium in the heart of Smyrna, and before the entire crowd, he prayed to God. Then they burned him at the stake for his faith in Christ. Early Christian writers tell us that as his body was consumed in flames, a supernatural demonstration of power came upon Polycarp, and he died in the power of God.

Polycarp may have died physically, but he lives on eternally in the presence of Christ. He didn't relinquish his faith, and even in the midst of the flames, he was an overcomer. And that is what God has called and equipped you to be too! This will be our focus for in our final lesson.

STUDY QUESTIONS

Study to shew thyself approved unto God, a workman that needeth not to be ashamed, rightly dividing the word of truth.
— 2 Timothy 2:15

1. Jesus said that for us to walk with Him, we will need to pick up our cross and follow Him. Take time to meditate on His words in Luke 9:23-25 as if Jesus was speaking directly to you. What do His words personally communicate to you? (Also consider Matthew 10:37-39; 16:24-26.)

2. After hearing the story of Polycarp, what inspires you most about his life? How does this encourage you in your personal walk of faith?

PRACTICAL APPLICATION

But be ye doers of the word, and not hearers only, deceiving your own selves.— James 1:22

1. In order for the believers in Smyrna to keep their jobs, they would have needed to compromise their commitment to Christ. Have you ever experienced a situation like this at work or among family members or friends? If so, take a moment to briefly share the situation.

2. The believers in Smyrna decided to discontinue their partnership with the pagan trade guilds. Instead of participating in ungodly practices, they honored their commitment to Christ. How about you? What decisions and actions have you made to navigate your difficult situation?

TOPIC

A Message to Overcoming Believers

SCRIPTURES

1. **Revelation 2:8-11** — And unto the angel of the church in Smyrna write; These things saith the first and the last, which was dead, and is alive; I know thy works, and tribulation, and poverty, (but thou art rich) and I know the blasphemy of them which say they are Jews, and are not, but are the synagogue of Satan. Fear none of those things which thou shalt suffer: behold, the devil shall cast some of you into prison, that ye may be tried; and ye shall have tribulation ten days: be thou faithful unto death, and I will give thee a crown of life. He that hath an ear, let him hear what the Spirit saith unto the churches; He that overcometh shall not be hurt of the second death.

GREEK WORDS

1. "I will give" — **δώσω** (*doso*): a future form of the Greek word *didomi*, which means *I give*, but in this verse could mean *I allow* or *I permit*

2. "crown" — **στέφανος** (*stephanos*): a victor's crown; in the ancient games, a laurel wreath was placed on the head of winning athletes; an athlete who obtained a victor's crown was esteemed and honored the rest of his life; the memories of his achievement were etched into society, ensuring that he would not be overlooked or forgotten during the balance of his life; it could be used in reference to any type of reward; the crown given to athletes, but most notably to runners after they had run their race or finished their contest victoriously

3. "overcometh" — **νικάω** (*nikao*): to overcome; pictures one who is overcoming; a victor, a champion, or one who possesses some type of superiority; can be translated to conquer, to defeat, to master, to overcome, to overwhelm, to surpass, or to be victorious; it was often used in Greek literature to portray athletes who had mastered their sport and ultimately reigned supreme as champions in the games; it could also describe a military victory of one foe against the other; to be permanently and consistently undeterred in one's efforts to over-

come and to obtain a lasting victory; can be translated to control, to conquer, to defeat, to master, to overcome, to overwhelm, to surpass, or to be victorious

4. "hurt" — ἀδικέω (*adikeo*): to harm, to hurt, or to injure

5. "second death" — θανάτου τοῦ δευτέρου (*thanatou tou deuterou*): death of the second kind

SYNOPSIS

The ancient city of Smyrna was once a magnificent city in the Roman province of Asia. Many historians believe it had a population of about 100,000 people during the time of the early New Testament when the church of Smyrna was first established. Yet people who professed faith in Christ were often dragged into the city stadium, the theater, or the open marketplace and publicly persecuted. They were beaten, stoned, and executed for their faith.

Jesus was personally aware of all that the believers were facing, including the abject poverty they were enduring day in and day out. In the midst of their misery, He spoke a message to the church of Smyrna, calling all Christians to be faithful and to overcome the attacks of the enemy. And everyone who endured to the end would win a victor's crown.

The emphasis of this lesson:

Believers in Smyrna faced severe persecution. Fueled by Satan himself, both the Jewish leaders and the pagans in the community attacked the Christians in Smyrna. But Jesus promised a crown of life to everyone who would stand on His Word and refuse to give in — regardless of what the enemy tried to do.

Jesus Spoke to the Pastor of the Church of Smyrna

In the second and third chapters of Revelation, Jesus spoke specialized messages to seven different churches: Ephesus, Smyrna, Pergamum, Thyatira, Sardis, Philadelphia, and Laodicea. In all seven cases, Jesus never directly addressed the church. Instead, He addressed the "angel" of each church. The word "angel" in all seven instances is the Greek word *angelos*. Although it can describe a Heaven-sent messenger, in these particular passages, it described *a special designated messenger* — the pastor of the church.

Jesus Himself had placed all seven of these pastors in their positions, and rather than ignore their place of authority, He honored it by speaking to them first. Jesus will never bypass the pastor's authority. He will always speak to him if He has something to say to the church — whether it be a word of correction or commendation. Then it is the pastor's responsibility to process the message and pass it on to the people in the congregation.

In Revelation 2:8 and 9, Jesus spoke to the angel, or pastor, of the church of Smyrna, saying, "…These things saith the first and the last, which was dead, and is alive; I know thy works, and tribulation, and poverty, (but thou art rich)…."

The Synagogue of Satan

Jesus continued in verse 9 saying, "…And I know the blasphemy of them which say they are Jews, and are not, but are the synagogue of Satan." The word "blasphemy" is taken from the Greek word *blasphemo*, which describes *vile speech or horrible, abusive language.* By using the word *blasphemo*, Jesus is telling us that the Jews were verbally abusing Christians. In fact, their behavior was so ungodly, He said they "say they are Jews, and are not, but are the synagogue of Satan."

Could anything worse be said of people who are supposed to be God's people? Jesus said they were of *the synagogue of Satan.* The word "Satan" is the Greek word *satanas,* which means *one who accuses, one who slanders, one who makes allegations.* This is what the Jews in Smyrna were doing — *accusing, slandering, and making allegations against the Christians in Smyrna.* They were speaking vile, abusive, blasphemous things about believers to the local pagan population.

Pagans believed that when something bad happened in their city, someone was to blame for it. For example, if there was a plague, it had to be because someone in this city did something wrong, and therefore, one of the gods sent the plague. If there was an earthquake, the gods were displeased and sent it as punishment because of the actions of a particular person or group in the city.

Although the Jewish leaders didn't believe in these gods, they knew that the pagans did, and they began to create suspicions and circulate rumors about the Christians in an effort to stir up the pagans against them. The Jews began to say things like, "You want to know why we had an earthquake? Do you want to know why we have had a crop failure? Do you want to know why this disease is spreading through the city? It's because of *the Christians*. They have upset the spiritual realm with their new, erroneous teaching. The Christians are the reason that curses, famines, wars, earthquakes, and sickness have come to our city." When the local pagan population began listening to these maligning accusations, they began to severely persecute the church.

Know That It's *Not* God Who Oppresses You

In Revelation 2:10, Jesus went on to say, "Fear none of those things which thou shalt suffer: behold, the devil shall cast some of you into prison...." The word "behold" is the Greek word *idou*, which carries the idea of *amazement, shock, and wonder*. It was as if Jesus was saying, "Wow! I'm amazed at what the devil is about to try to do to you."

One of the things that most amazed Jesus was that the level of opposition coming against the believers. It wasn't just a little demonic activity. It was an all-out assault brought on by the devil himself. The Greek structure of this verse includes the definite article, indicating it was *the* devil who was about to wreak havoc against the church of Smyrna.

Many times when Christians hear the word "tried," they automatically think that God is somehow behind what is happening. However, that is an inaccurate view. This verse clearly states it was *the devil* who "tried" the believers in Smyrna, not God. It was *the devil* that caused them to lose their jobs. It was *the devil* that caused their finances and resources to dry up. And it was *the devil* that thrust them into poverty and prison. It was *not* God!

Revelation 2:10 says, "...Behold, *the devil* shall cast some of you into prison, that ye may be *tried*...." The word "tried" is the Greek word *peiradzo*, which means *to test*. It describes *a calculated test deliberately designed to expose any deficiency and break a person.*

The believers in Smyrna had declared Jesus to be Lord of their lives. They had surrendered themselves to Him and even been willing to walk away from their jobs to avoid corrupting themselves in pagan activities. In response, the devil devised a calculated test to see just how serious they were about serving Christ. Would they give up and return to the trade guilds to secure work? Or would they remain faithful to Christ?

Jesus told the church of Smyrna, "…And ye shall have tribulation ten days…" (Revelation 2:9). This word "tribulation" is the Greek word *thlipsis*, which describes *a high-pressure situation that is crushing, debilitating, or overpowering*. Jesus didn't pretend everything was going to be fine. He told them that trouble was coming, but then He said it would be for "ten days." Although prophetically, this likely referred to the ten Roman emperors who persecuted the Church, it essentially meant that it wouldn't last very long.

If you are going through a tough time, realize that it won't last. *This too shall pass*. The devil thinks he is going to destroy you, but he won't. Once you emerge on the other side, you will come out as pure gold.

Practice Being Faithful

After Jesus forewarned the church of Smyrna about what they would face, He told them, "…Be thou faithful unto death, and I will give thee a crown of life" (Revelation 2:10). The phrase "be thou" is the Greek word *ginomai*, which means *to become*. It depicts *a process of becoming*. This could actually be translated, "Be thou *in the process of becoming* faithful unto death." That is, "Start where you are and begin practicing faithfulness today."

Jesus was telling these believers — and us — to be faithful, regardless of the price. Don't give up or surrender your position. The Kingdom of God is at stake. "Be thou faithful" means start practicing faithfulness today, and don't worry that you're not going to be faithful in a difficult moment. If you will begin practicing faithfulness today, tomorrow, and the next day, and the day after that, and so forth, when you face a difficult problem, it won't be so difficult because you will have constructed the characteristic of faithfulness into your entire being.

Receive a Crown From Christ Himself

What was the reward for being faithful unto death? Jesus said, "I will give thee a crown of life." The phrase "I will give thee" is from the Greek word *doso*. It is a future form of the Greek word *didomi*, which means *I will give*. Jesus was describing a future moment when He would personally bestow a crown to believers who endure to the end. This promise was not only for the faithful Christians in Smyrna, but also to faithful Christians of all generations.

The word "crown" is the Greek word *stephanos*, and it describes *a victor's crown*. In the ancient games, a laurel wreath was placed on the head of winning athletes. An athlete who obtained a victor's crown was esteemed and honored the rest of his life. The memories of his achievements were etched into society, ensuring that he would not be overlooked or forgotten during the balance of his life. The word crown could be used in reference to any type of reward, but it primarily depicted the crown given to athletes who finished their contest victoriously.

When Jesus says, "I will give you a crown of life," the implication is that you're an athlete running in a race, and this is your moment to fight. If you'll fight to the end gloriously, refusing to give up, when your contest is over, Jesus, the Judge of the games Himself, will come forward and put a crown on your head to reward you for what you have done and for how you fought the fight of faith. Could there be any greater reward than Jesus personally crowning you and saying, "Well done, thou good and faithful servant"!

Five Different Crowns

The New Testament talks about five specific crowns that will be given out as rewards. In First Corinthians 9:25, we see that there's a crown called the "crown of incorruption." This one will be given to individuals who developed and mastered temperance, which is discipline and self-control.

First Thessalonians 2:19 reveals a second crown called the "crown of rejoicing." Scholars have also identified this one as the "soul-winner's crown." For those who regularly share the Good News and lead people to Christ, a special crown is being crafted as their reward.

The Bible also describes a third crown in Second Timothy 4:8 called the "crown of righteousness." This is a special crown which will be given to people who eagerly awaited and anticipated Jesus' next coming.

Then in First Peter 5:4, a fourth crown is mentioned, and it is called the "crown of glory." This award is sometimes called the "shepherd's crown" or the "pastor's crown." It's a special reward that will be placed upon the heads of pastors who faithfully fulfilled their function.

The fifth crown identified in Scripture is the "crown of life," which we saw in Revelation 2:10, and it is also found in James 1:12. The "crown of life," also called the "martyr's crown," is a high honor that will be given to those who died for their faith, who suffered persecution, or who experienced martyrdom on some level because of their devotion to Jesus.

These are the five specific crowns that will be rewarded to those who run their race to win.

What It Means To Be an Overcomer

Jesus declared in Revelation 2:11, "He that hath an ear, let him hear what the Spirit saith unto the churches; He that overcometh shall not be hurt of the second death." The word "overcometh" is the Greek word *nikao*, and it pictures *one who is overcoming*. This person is constantly in the process of overcoming. This overcomer is *a victor, a champion, or one who possesses some type of superiority*. This word "overcometh" can also be translated *to conquer, to defeat, to master, to overcome, to overwhelm, to surpass, or to be victorious*.

The word *nikao* was often used in Greek literature to portray athletes who had mastered their sport and ultimately reigned supreme as champions in the games. It could also describe *a military victory of one foe against the other*. It carries the idea of *being permanently and consistently undeterred in one's efforts to overcome and to obtain a lasting victory*. The word *nikao* can also be translated *to control, to conquer, to defeat, to master, to overcome, to overwhelm, to surpass, or to be victorious*.

Being an overcomer is not tied to a single action or event. It is a way of life. Overcoming is a mindset or an attitude that says, *"I'm not giving up, and I'm not budging. I'm going to conquer my enemies, and I'm not stopping until all of them are under my feet and I've done what God has told me to do."*

This is what it means to be an overcomer, and with the Holy Spirit living inside of you, you've got what it takes to live an overcoming life.

STUDY QUESTIONS

Study to shew thyself approved unto God, a workman that needeth not to be ashamed, rightly dividing the word of truth.
— 2 Timothy 2:15

1. Jesus made it clear in John 16:33 that in this life we will have tribulation. Although very few of us actually *want* trouble, God will use it to cause us to overcome and to do some amazing things in our lives. Read Deuteronomy 8:2-6 and James 1:2-4 and identify how God

will turn tests you go through into testimonies and will produce an overcoming mindset in you besides!

2. When we are *tried* by the enemy, we are often tempted to *act* like the enemy and give in to what he wants for our lives. Carefully meditate on James 1:13-17 and write what the Holy Spirit shows you about the source of temptation and the source of blessings.

PRACTICAL APPLICATION

But be ye doers of the word, and not hearers only, deceiving your own selves.
— James 1:22

1. When you hear the word "tried," do you automatically think that God is somehow behind what is happening? If not, what do you think? How has this lesson given you a more positive perspective of trials?

2. Close your eyes and imagine standing in the throne room of Heaven, and Jesus is directly in front of you. In an instant, high-definition footage of your life begins to play on celestial screens. Suddenly, the King of kings calls your name and asks you to step forward. How do you think you would respond? What crown(s) might you hope to receive?

A Prayer To Receive Salvation

If you've never received Jesus as your Savior and Lord, now is the time for you to experience the new life Jesus wants to give you! To receive God's gift of salvation that can be obtained through Jesus alone, pray this prayer from your heart:

> *Jesus, I repent of my sin and receive You as my Savior and Lord. Wash away my sin with Your precious blood and make me completely new. I thank You that my sin is removed, and Satan no longer has any right to lay claim on me. Through Your empowering grace, I faithfully promise that I will serve You as my Lord for the rest of my life.*

If you just prayed this prayer of salvation, you are born again! You are a brand-new creation in Christ! Would you please let us know of your decision by going to **renner.org/salvation**? We would love to connect with you and pray for you as you begin your new life in Christ.

Scriptures for further study: John 3:16; John 14:6; Acts 4:12; Ephesians 1:7; Hebrews 10:19,20; 1 Peter 1:18,19; Romans 10:9,10; Colossians 1:13; 2 Corinthians 5:17; Romans 6:4; 1 Peter 1:3

Notes

Notes

Notes

CLAIM YOUR FREE RESOURCE!

As a way of introducing you further to the teaching ministry of Rick Renner, we would like to send you FREE of charge his teaching, "How To Receive a Miraculous Touch From God" on CD or as an MP3 download.

In His earthly ministry, Jesus commonly healed *all* who were sick of *all* their diseases. In this profound message, learn about the manifold dimensions of Christ's wisdom, goodness, power, and love toward all humanity who came to Him in faith with their needs.

☑ **YES, I want to receive Rick Renner's monthly teaching letter!**

Simply scan the QR code to claim this resource or go to: **renner.org/claim-your-free-offer**

Connect WITH US!